AFETO

MARIA STRAW-ÇINAR
with illustrations by
LITO SILVA

Author biography

Maria Straw-Çinar is a poet,writer and teacher.Her debut novel *Girl,* was short-listed for the Cinnamon Press Novella award and is available to purchase online. In 2016 she published a poetry collection, *Flamenco* with Lulu Press, and her play, *Vinegar Alley,* was long-listed for the Papatango Writing Prize. She has been inspired by the work of artist Lito Silva to create this ekphrastic poetry collection, *Afeto.* You can find more of her work on Poetry and Other Pleasures mstrawcinar.wordpress.com

A note on the illustrator

Lito Silva was born in Lisbon in 1979 and grew up in Cape Verde. He moved to London when he was 21 and now lives and works there. He began painting in 2009 and had his first exhibition in Casa de Morna, Lisbon, followed by a major international exhibition in 2010 at Art Algarve. He participated in the London-based cultural festival, 'Amazing Africa' in 2010 and his work was exhibited at The Royal Commonwealth Society in 2011. This resulted in being invited to attend an Observance for Commonwealth Day in the presence of Her Majesty, The Queen and His Royal highness, Prince Philip, duke of Edinburgh. Lito Silva identifies himself as a self-taught artist who expresses himself through art in oil paintings with warm, strong colours resembling his upbringing in Africa. He dreams of learning with the great masters and travelling to share his culture and art to help and inspire young people.

Supported using public funding by

ARTS COUNCIL ENGLAND

Contents

Afeto

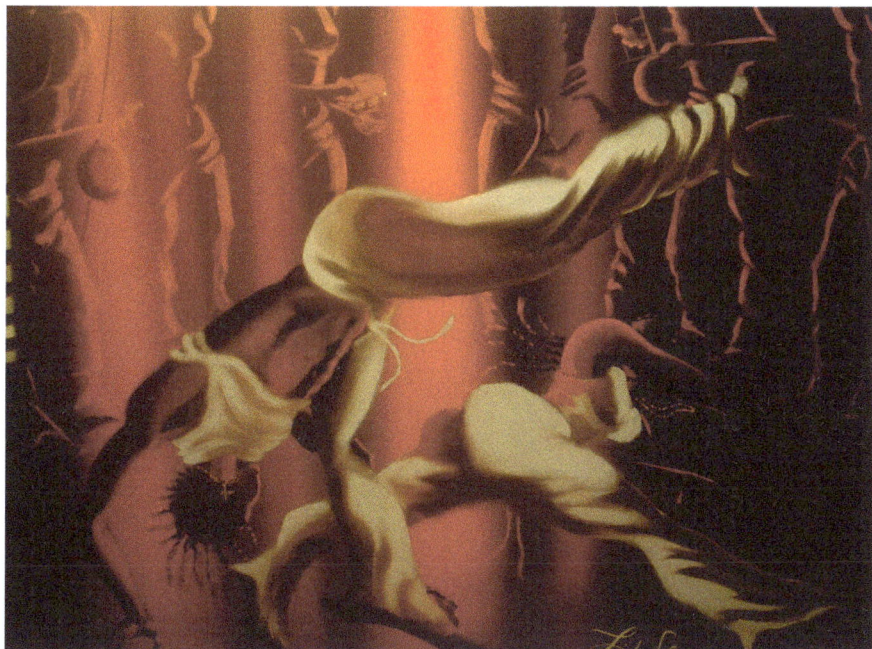

Master of the Dance

Hidden in history's huts,
        the beat rises—
hands become drums,
    servants master their bodies
        manoeuvre and slide secret
          coded *rodas* to
            free the slaveself
              from shackles

break the Cakewalk
          topping of sugarsweet
            blackgold sold to stiffen
                    the upper lip

Fight dance macabre
     out of huts of history
        flappers flap,
          plantations slap slaves
       slap back, dance as
           the whip cracks-a-way
      smacks the Black Bottom
        with Charleston flicks as
          Lindy hopping white women
            kick away pencil thin lives.

      hands clapping, rapping rhythms of life…

slavemaster stabs a steak through
     cardinal dancing hearts—
       take his clothes, strip his soul
        stomp him down; but his burnet
          blanket shining skin bounds and leaps
            frisks and frolicks,   kicks and screams
Gene Kelly *singing in the rain*
     came from slave pain.

Caporeira do you dare
     dance in shadowlight
       cat-like whips and hisses,
         razor blades grasped tightly,
silvery toes glint and strike
     fork-lightning flashes—
       slashed in a blink of an eye
         slaveprints shape new skies

Now the slavemaster's blighted
　　　blackgold crops fight back.
It's just a dance
　　　dance, swish, kick
　　　　　fat cat owl sees no pussy cat now,
　　　　　　twisted purrs,
contorted Houdini escapees
　　　find the key,
　　　　　hips slash and sway
　　　　　　as the juke box plays—
like last summer.

Language divides, bodies collide
　　　in connecting ecstasy
　　　　　and secret silent wars
　　　　　　masters swore to stop—
Achilles heel cut;
　　　　　Let them never dance again.

…
And the masters sit on porches,
cocks in the hoop,
sundowner drinks clink,
night's auric rush
　　　　　sinks into sheltering sky

Yet faintly, in the distance
of deadly blackgold skies,
a sound that never ceases,
urgent as the first-
　　　　　　born's heartbeat,
　　　still, the tap tap tap,
　　　　drumming, endless thumbing
　　　　　rolling spools of memory—
　　　　　　the slave dance springs
　　　　　　　eternal, blossoming heat of life—

a drum a drum
the slave doth come.

9

Nossa Infancia

Skimming hoops, skidding stones, new bones frizz with glory pinging
round the china bowl days that glisten like glarneys,
voices hollowing out the sky, then home to motherlove, bedded and
warm;lying looking at the stars, diamond punched bliss, Mama's tender kiss
wrapping up the night—mandarin sunbeams awaken sleepy bye eyes—
flutters of pencil-sharpenings curling, unfurling to flight;
a whisper of moths heading for light,

tongues not yet tied announce all they see, tulip lips, sharp and sweet
as lemony wine, taste symphonies planted deep down in memory;
new knees skinned—drops of blood splash sorrel sands like raspberry
tarts laughter stretches apricot sky, fills air with dew no adult can crush,
quash, quell—belly laughs spiral and swell rubious apple peels
helicoptering heavens, airborne howls and roars of joy bodyshaking
delights, vibrate and quake the earth's erythraean core.

Oh! Cracked and spider-veined planet, rejoice in these tiny taps on
your stilton-bruised brain; head cut—scarred indelible, keep running,
                                        into forever, unstoppable.

Hot heat Jazz

Call and response notes float over killing fields,
spiritual stories—nuggets of blackgold
boldy hollered across snowy cotton fields,
sound of music hanging in air laying bare
                              a hard day's nightache

Rising from rags in time into the mix, European clicks
Irish jigs, German waltzes, French quadrilles
New Orleans schmaltz and sass
                              all that jazz
Ragtime!
Flappers chop their hair
Americans throw caution...
swing to new rhythm,
synchronicity glides,
shades of blue
Gillespie-life fizzy
notes spinning ol'
black magic Dizzy,
and the dancehall born,
till wartorn cries screech
down time's elevator shafts,

a man with no notion of rhyme—
rises up speaking guttural,
drowning out music
and the dance halls close,
all the good players
shipped off to die—
them white folk found no one
to make dance hall songs fly,

but the beboppers gathered
listening to intricate sounds
strain as the moustachioed man
manically barked hate
spewed pain—
notes in the gutter,
yet music tinkles in stars.

Bebop to freedom,
Monk obeys scatting,
free chatting,
scatterbrain natting
Thelonius speeds up the music,
too fast for dance.
From fingers to brain—
Blitzing warpain
Blues fuses with jazz.

Out of smoke-choked bars notes rise, drift across plains
once again, sweat drops drip onto white cotton-
picking fields, melodies drift back, drift forth; so gentle,
so sweet, clever and fulsome and deep.
Oh, those hot steamy nights—
                              nights that jazz was born.

Nossa Danca
(Our Dance)

Semi-quavers quiver
bent-double
on the dancefloor,
tender is the night,
moonlit bodies bob
with the current,
treble cleft hearts
spin solo, all souls
now one—

punctuated movement,
semi-colonials of the night's
exclamations, abbreviations—

a ricochet of notes
slip slyly away
from the saxophone's
crushed crescendos—
midnight's ellipsis...
bodies curve
quotation marks
leaning towards their
future

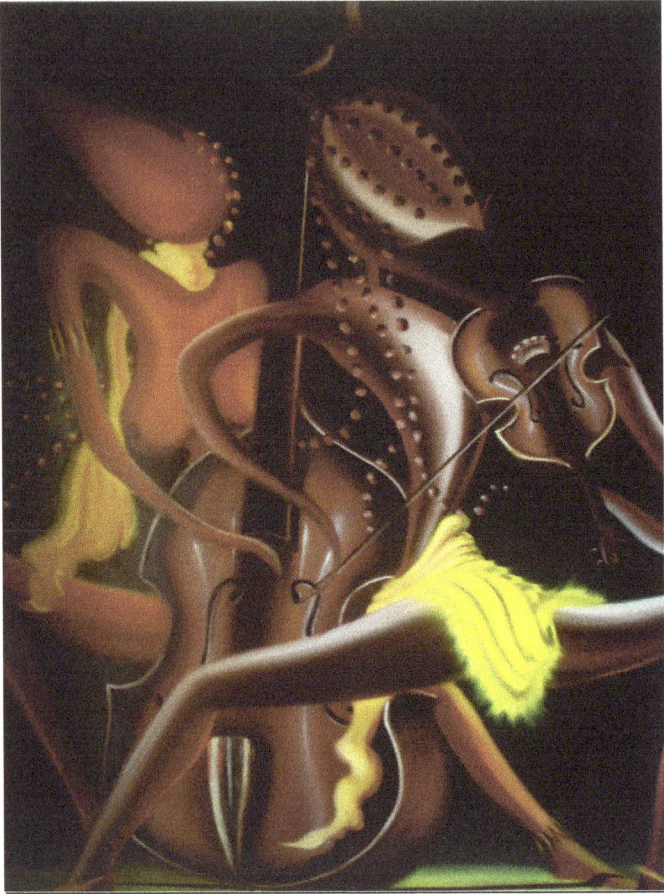

The fantasy of music

Lost in music
gone far far away
in the bottle
of forgetting
and remembering.
Letters blowing
in the wind.
Fragments, notes
trigger memories
of hope and sand
in my eyes.
A moondance
promise over
dusty horizon,
sunset drinks
glisten night
into all it is
promised to be.
You and I
and the fantasy
of music
until we die.
You and I
dancing,
twisting naked
in the bare villa,
drunk and blind—
Love, love, love,
drink and dance
for tomorrow
we shall die.

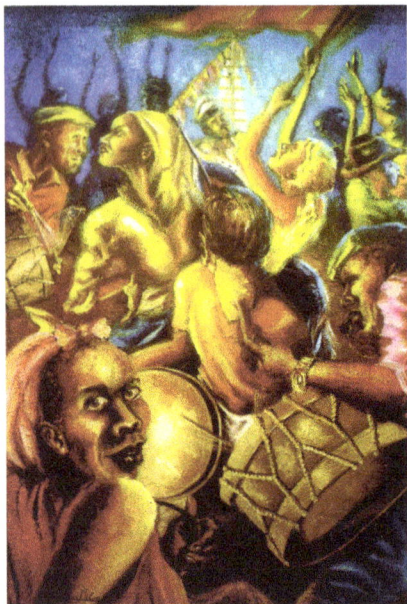

Suadade

From acid to blues,
　　retro to smooth —
Fado, tango, morna,
　　rumba rubs along
travels to Cape Verde
　　where the the blues
　　　　　　is　called Suadade; longing —
　　　　　　fuses loss and love.

Suadade-love remains
　　when the lover has gone —
　　　　　　imprints in rhyme.
　　　　　　　　landscapes in time

since music be …
　　　　　　Play on…

The Afternoon

Sun rays burn holes in day,
men play cards with hearts
shuffled by rough fingers
guitar strings pluck
diamonds from last
night's fires,

the afternoon club sings
of the wrongs done
by spades dug
too deep,

touching nerves, breaking bones;
in this happy hinterland
basked in swollen light
sit these old Adams,
friends for life,
suspending,
night from
day

come what may
they know
there are
other
ways
to
die

The Fishermen

Early dawn chartreuse,
crustaceans stretch, shell-beds
shudder, cushioned by seas,
old men's fisheyes
flick open, pearly grey,
skeletons rattle in sea-boned
closets, skulls and crosses
invocate moonlight fires—

The fish rise too,
silver-gill breathe
waxes and wanes;
opalescent foils
hook dawn deaths,
sounds of skiffs
swallowing whole shoals,
snare netted.

A lone swordfish—
morning basking
in sulphurous sun;
jetblack moon-eyes
shadowed by
death's last post

dawn sweats and shifts—

here come the fishermen,
harpoon's heroes'
spearing fleshwounds
into the vast blue silver;
target thrashes,
fins spin, plummet toward
unshallow grave,
longsword impales the ocean floor;
carrion calls to bed, to bed
floods bloodstreams
across the coast.

Fisherman's veins pop and rise
erected at the catch—
lifekill.

Afeto

slit-moonfruit, slippery skin
hardens, pips and seed
bleed this quiet room
hanging bat blind as
curled up grace,
two-faced twin—
dreams in waiting

inside the cave walls
lingering with intent
lallygags this bodydouble,
cyclopic seahorse
with one-eye on the prize,
scaffolding skin shapes—
cutcake moulds
blasted in the
ancient kiln

moon into sun,
then a cry—
a sound so old
swelling up from the earth
that first O
now broken.
the division
is done.

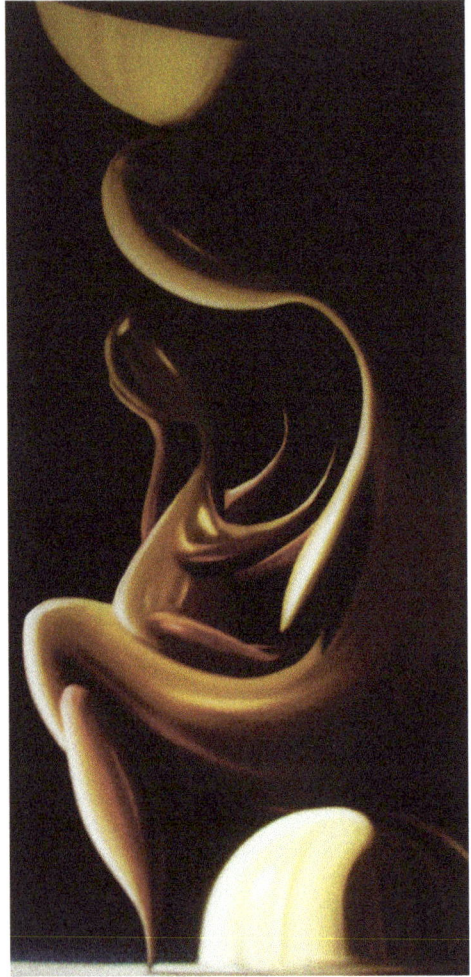

A Caminhada
(The Walk)

Sunset squirts squid-ink
across the sky, flavescent flames,
ready to burst, scald underfoot

Huntress strides gigantic; burning
gemstone horizons, soft soles follow,
branding tiny footprints
on her heart

Blood-streaked eyes mesmerise Mama Africa
perpetually parched—Jurassic thirst,
suckled and quenched.

Goddess;
split fruit woman
see-far woman

Mama Africa

Where do I begin? Where did it begin?
O, Mama Africa, Grandmother of the world,
continents held in your arms where life began,
dinosaurs strode the earth, one greatland Mother,
no borders, smashed by an asteroid—snaked into human life.

O Mama Africa, hear my prayer:
Bandage the world or my eyes, teach boys manners maketh man,
from woman they came—teach them
                    from woman they came
                            from women they come

O Mama Africa, wipe my tears,
diamond dogs bark in the huts
of war-torn places where men make faces at the world
And still the women and childgirls suffer.

Scar clan

O Mama Africa, unstitch these terrors.
let the girlchild cry in pleasure and women walk safely.
Hold us close as your smile heals the shame,
let the last blazing sunstar in the sky
                            shine on the world.

O Mama Africa, only you know the truth,
sing us life's tune—as you caress sable skin,
hazelnut moons; a world without sin

O Mama Africa, squeeze the world
until all drops of hate
evaporate gently
And only love
Only love
Only
Love
O

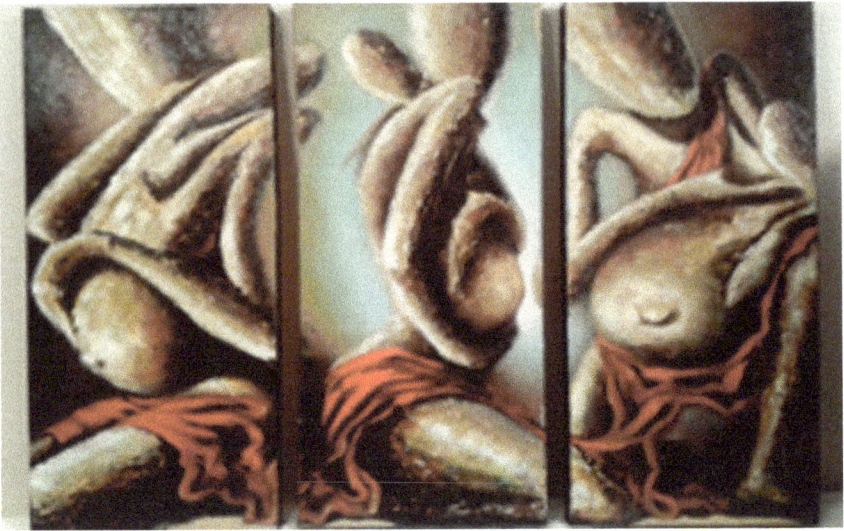

Eden

In the beginning…Him
formless and empty
dusted off Man
lying beneath the Knowledge Tree
tossed a spare rib
to seed a woman
skin and blistered
Soon they knew
flat-bellied serpent
forked tongue stung,
tied and muted
a couple of swells
damned in time.

Him.

And in the end, she,
cow-heft , colossal
taut as a drum,
face-lifted
ready for the final fling—
ribs, hips and bone
shift and flood
uncrumpling life,
canyon echoes
hang in her hair—

Her.

The Exchange

Mum, bird-like, vulnerable,
slain by this raw war,
wheeled around like cargo
on the way to X-ray,
hell's waiting room,
the cavernous lift-mouth
ready to swallow you whole,
slowly, you turn and smile,
wry-eyed trickster
stroking my belly
with your soft-punctured hands,
you're on the way in,
you whisper through my skin:
I'm on my way out.

Flashbulb blasts,
cancerous illuminations
ignite the fallow field,
chemo's dread shots,
death's decoy
phosphorous pin-pricks
devouring your insides.
                    And then you…

Your hand flutters inside,
butterfly fingers flicker
your still beating heart
ta ra pa pum pum
urgent, pulsating me
and my drum desperate
to be known,

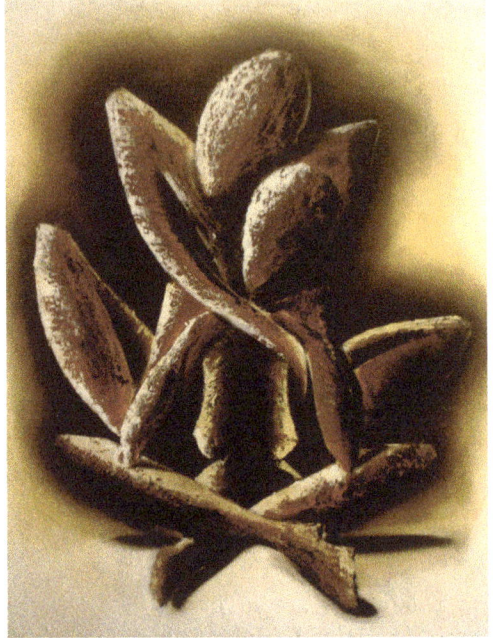

the swamp-like scan
revealing tiny limb
and bone, acrobatic
tumbler in the spin
                of life

this is the spirit world
and all the monitors
in this whitecure-scape
cannot fathom
            the depths
                    we feel.

Middle Earth

Mother, the face of all roots—
middle-aged-birthers need their Mothers,
Mama now themselves, Primigravida, later Mater;
childlike until Mother's hood darkens the path,
no book to show the way—middle-earth Mother
neither here nor there, freedom gone
along with Mother's love, now you are the Mother,
but know not what you do, middle-earthed,
the child and the ancient pull both ways
as baby cries for you, just you,
but who can you cry to
only the empty space
the lost place
shaped
Mother

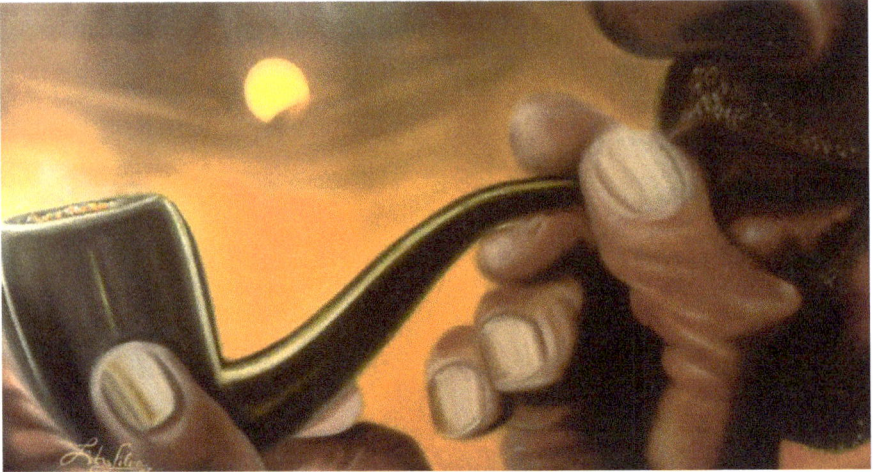

Pipe Dreams

I heard the news today:
young homeless girl,
open-mouthed, smiling
at the cold dawn hour—
frozen to death.
Burnt matches all around.

Shipped to London streets, paved with Hatton garden gold, diamonds flash past, wedged onto pudgy rollicking hands, the matchgirl settles in her spot, glacial winds needle her skin, deep in her pocket, she grasps the golden matchbox, grandfather's gift—

to keep you warm in that cold town.

What do you see my little one?
Make a picture, tell a story.
Can you see the choo choo train
puffing doughnut rings,
into the periwinkle sky,
put your finger through the hole—

one day you shall be wed.
Her father dead, this is where her path led—cinereous streets of London,
fog-cloaked air chokes glaucous light, broken little matchgirl strikes,
haloes of smoke hover over her head—

Vovo!
Grandpapa's smile ignites,
pipe flumes burn the night—
the kindest man puts a shell to her ear—
Oceans of comfort—*ssh, ssh, ssh...*

Yet here by the rivers of Lethe, the biting wind cuts raw, arctic slices
prick n' snip the vinegary night. Jack Frost, Ripper or Jones—shadowy
monsters own the night—men not ogres, but necrophiliac men, prey on
the weak, looking to turn girlflesh into gold—in scabby bedsits,
spattered across the city.

She fumbles fingers and thumbs, strikes a match—

in the puffs of cloud,
Papapom smiles:
Vovo! Vovo!
Wheeeeeeeeeee!
My tiny puffafish girl,
love of my life …

this face she scaled so many times
warm craggy wrinkles—
deep ridges of a life well-borne ...

flame flickers and stings,
ice-blue numbness clots her eyes;
purple fingers spread
—jacaranda blossom
reaching for the moon—
phosphorus night breath.

29

coconut girl, throw down another icicle—
rain-stalactites pelt down,
she raises her head, her tongue
a helter-skelter of desire
lashings of coconut juice
cascade earthwards,

VOVO!
My little pumpkin,
come try this,
Vovo! Let us sup!

she slides smoothly
down his chocolate pipe
into giant sandpaper hands
her frozen fingers reaching
for that fat old sun

Drink my little angel
drink every last drop
come with me
to paradise

I heard the news today
young homeless girl frozen to death—
must have been trying to warm herself.

Roots of Love

Pushing down into forever
embedded in the soil's soul
rooted in histories of love
We are made from clay
the earth creaks as your love shifts
planets collide to the sound of your kiss
where does it come from?

You give me edible glitter made of stars
awakening spasms of spangled dust
silver-swarm fallout
(ashes) lain dormant for years
We are magnificent

Splayed and slopped in the dirt
we root our pleasure into perfect skin
and bones, set in stone
like two muddied gods
wrestling in the dark
bloodhounds of love
listening to the earth's beating heart
We are magnificent

Searing of the roots
earthquakes shake us—
Mercury forces us back
erases the oceans,
ravages the forests
the mad moon is pulling
the roots from the trees.

We were once magnificent.

A-feto

tiny dragon flames,
keying our aurum hearts
wail rises
bloating air
balloons a-fresh
dawnstrains
newly
born
a-feto

9 781788 640350